Animals in My Yard

Eagles

by Amy McDonald

BELLWETHER MEDIA • MINNEAPOLIS, MN

Blastoff! Beginners are developed by literacy experts and educators to meet the needs of early readers. These engaging informational texts support young children as they begin reading about their world. Through simple language and high frequency words paired with crisp, colorful photos, Blastoff! Beginners launch young readers into the universe of independent reading.

Sight Words in This Book 🔍

a	in	the	up
and	it	they	use
big	long	this	what
down	make	three	
good	on	time	
have	see	to	

This edition first published in 2022 by Bellwether Media, Inc.

No part of this publication may be reproduced in whole or in part without written permission of the publisher. For information regarding permission, write to Bellwether Media, Inc., Attention: Permissions Department, 6012 Blue Circle Drive, Minnetonka, MN 55343.

Library of Congress Cataloging-in-Publication Data

Names: McDonald, Amy, author.
Title: Eagles / by Amy McDonald.
Description: Minneapolis, MN : Bellwether Media, 2022. | Series: Animals in my yard | Includes bibliographical references and index. | Audience: Ages 4-7 | Audience: Grades K-1
Identifiers: LCCN 2021040733 (print) | LCCN 2021040734 (ebook) | ISBN 9781644875629 (library binding) | ISBN 9781648345739 (ebook)
Subjects: LCSH: Eagles--Juvenile literature.
Classification: LCC QL696.F32 M354 2022 (print) | LCC QL696.F32 (ebook) | DDC 598.9/42--dc23
LC record available at https://lccn.loc.gov/2021040733
LC ebook record available at https://lccn.loc.gov/2021040734

Text copyright © 2022 by Bellwether Media, Inc. BLASTOFF! BEGINNERS and associated logos are trademarks and/or registered trademarks of Bellwether Media, Inc.

Editor: Betsy Rathburn   Designer: Brittany McIntosh

Printed in the United States of America, North Mankato, MN.

Table of Contents

Eagles!	4
Body Parts	6
The Lives of Eagles	12
Eagle Facts	22
Glossary	23
To Learn More	24
Index	24

Eagles!

What a BIG nest!
Hello, eagles!

nest

Body Parts

Eagles have **talons**. They hold on tight.

talons

Eagles have **hooked beaks**. They grab food.

hooked beak

Eagles have wide wings. They fly and dive!

The Lives of Eagles

Eagles make nests in trees. They use long sticks.

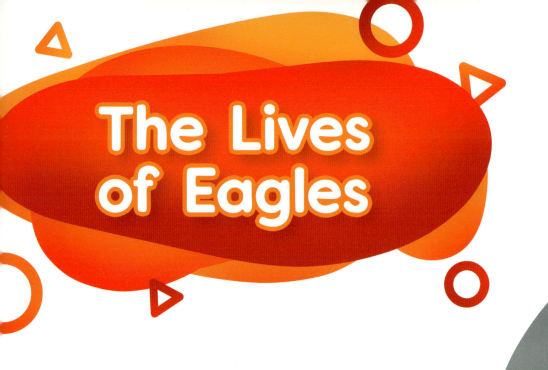

They lay up to three eggs in the nest.

eggs

Eagles fly to hunt. They have good eyes to spot **prey**.

fish

eye

birds

rabbits

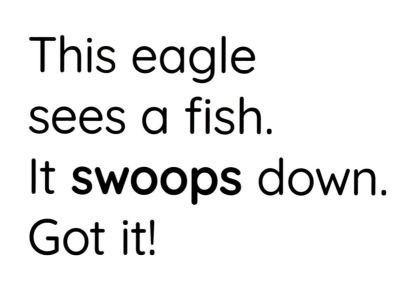

This eagle sees a fish.
It **swoops** down.
Got it!

The eagle brings meat back to the nest. Dinner time!

Eagle Facts

Eagle Body Parts

wings

hooked beak

talons

Eagle Food

fish

birds

rabbits

Glossary

hooked beaks

the mouths of some birds that curve down

prey

animals that are hunted

swoops

flies down quickly

talons

claws on a bird

To Learn More

ON THE WEB

FACTSURFER

Factsurfer.com gives you a safe, fun way to find more information.

1. Go to www.factsurfer.com.

2. Enter "eagles" into the search box and click 🔍.

3. Select your book cover to see a list of related content.

Index

dive, 10
eggs, 14
eyes, 16, 17
fish, 16, 18
fly, 10, 16
food, 8
hooked beaks, 8, 9
hunt, 16

meat, 20
nest, 4, 5, 12, 14, 20
prey, 16
sticks, 12
swoops, 18
talons, 6
trees, 12
wings, 10, 11

The images in this book are reproduced through the courtesy of: Eric Isselee, front cover; Aleksei Andreev, p. 3; BirdImages, pp. 5, 21; YK, p. 6; Svitlana Tkach, p. 7; Michal Ninger, p. 9; critterbiz, p. 11; Frank Fichtmueller, p. 13; Lori Skelton, p. 14; Martin Smart/ Alamy, p. 15; karamysh, p. 16; Vladimir Kogan Michael, p. 17 (top); Sean Xu, p. 17 (bottom left); Tom Reichner, p. 17 (bottom right); Jeffry Weymier, p. 19; Serjio74, p. 22; Ian Dewar Photography, p. 22 (fish); Maria Dryfhout/ Alamy, p. 22 (birds); Zoonar GmbH/ Alamy, p. 22 (rabbits); Anahita Daklani, p. 23 (hooked beaks); Vasik Olga, p. 23 (prey); FloridaStock, p. 23 (swoops); Alexandre Boudet, p. 23 (talons).